contents

foreword

There are few issues as fundamental yet overlooked as menstrual health and period equity. Constantly shrouded in stigma, menstruation is looked upon by many as a "taboo" topic, leaving the subset of issues surrounding it often unaddressed. The works curated for this publication serve as a testament to the ongoing struggle for menstruators' rights and autonomy worldwide, a reminder that their voices deserve to be heard, and a call to action towards lifting the stigma shrouding it.

Through diverse mediums and perspectives, these pieces illuminate the multifaceted dimensions of menstruation—from its biological significance to its cultural and social implications. Additionally, these artworks challenge taboos surrounding menstruation, inviting us to confront and dismantle them. This publication spotlights artists whose creativity serves as a vessel of expression and catalyst for change. It is an invitation to dialogue, reflection, and action—a reminder that the pursuit of gender equality must include addressing the most fundamental aspects of bodily autonomy.

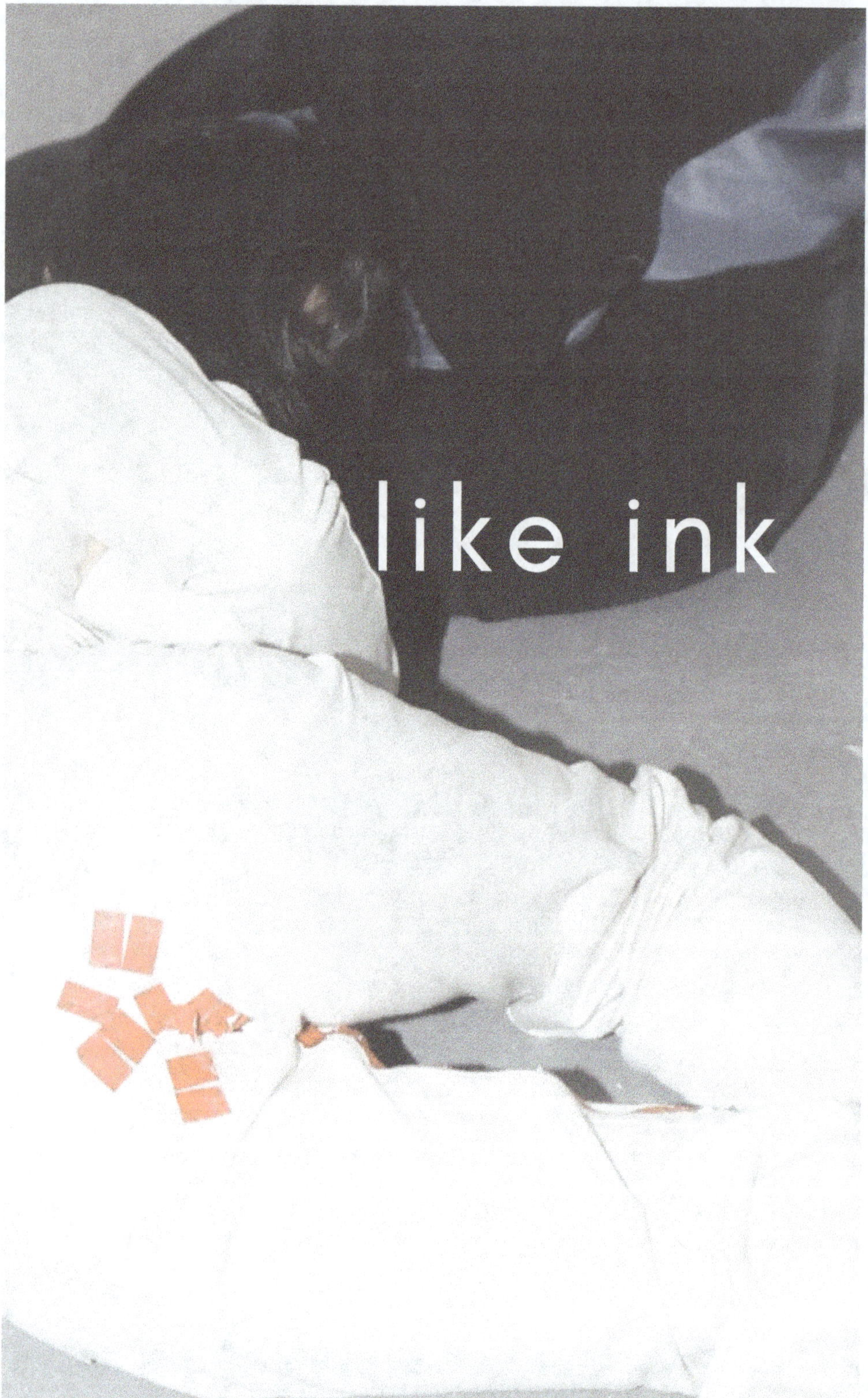
like ink

like ink

"like ink" explores menstruation not just as a biological phenomenon, but as a profound human experience marked by physical and emotional complexities.

As part of "like ink", artists delve into the nuances of menstrual and female reproductive health, pain, illness and the societal narratives that shape our understanding of these issues.

Through their diverse perspectives and creative expressions, they illuminate the somewhat stigmatized aspects of menstruation, inviting reflection, empathy, and dialogue on a topic central to menstruators' lives worldwide.

Menstruation is not just a biological process, it is a powerful and profound experience that connects us to the cycles of nature and the rhythms of our own bodies.

Maisie Hill

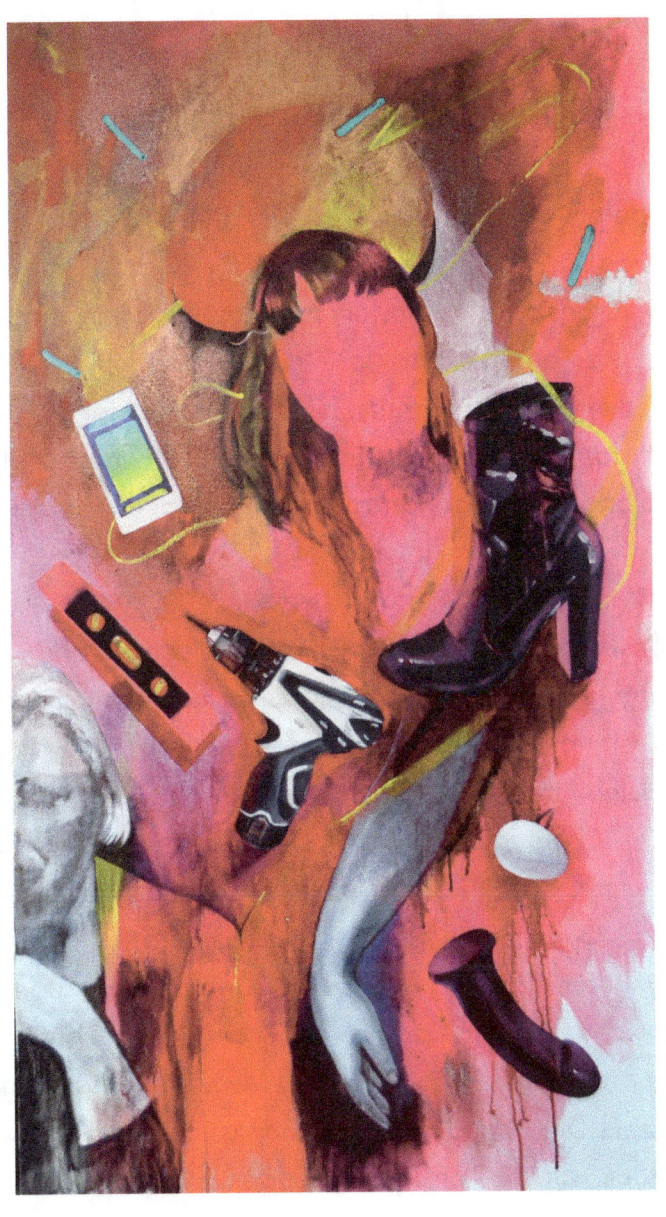

Wolensky, Meg. (2022). Halo Breaking, [oil and graphite on canvas]

Originally from West Chester, Pennsylvania, Meg Wolensky is a queer nonbinary visual artist based in Philadelphia. Meg performs painting as a healing practice for queer community as they recover from C-PTSD, translating colorful fragments of experiences, memories, and dreams into a cohesive whole that is reflective of queer identity, history, and resistance. These investigative collage-like paintings layer cross-sections of colorful personal narrative, trompe-l'oeil objects, and indicators of time as it whips by.

Wolensky's work has been exhibited in venues across the country, including Drexel University, Kutztown University, University of Southern Mississippi, Moore College of Art & Design, the Pennsylvania Academy of the Fine Arts (PAFA), Woodmere Art Museum, InLiquid Gallery, Seraphin Gallery, Rodger LaPelle Galleries, William Way LGBT Community Center, Democratic National Convention, Painted Bride Art Center, Abington Art Center, the Banana Factory Arts & Education Center and many more. in 2023, Wolensky was the recipient of InLiquid's Dina Wind Fellowship by a jury of outstanding curators, artists, and arts leaders from around the Greater Philadelphia area.

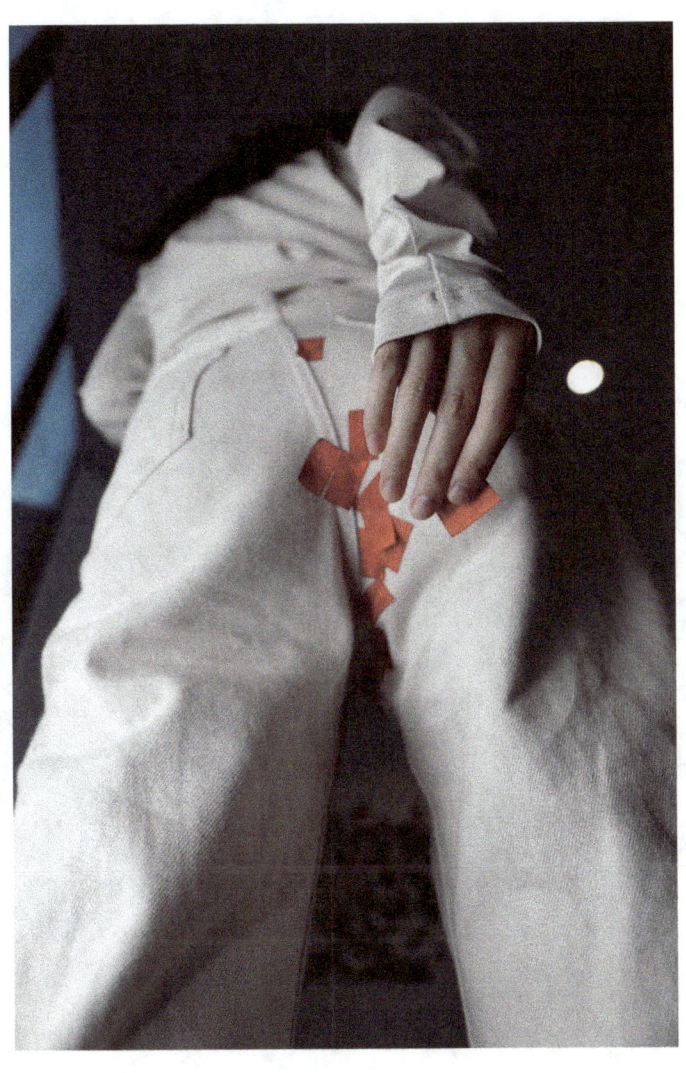

Yuying, Huang, (2023). Monthly, [photography (performance documentation)]

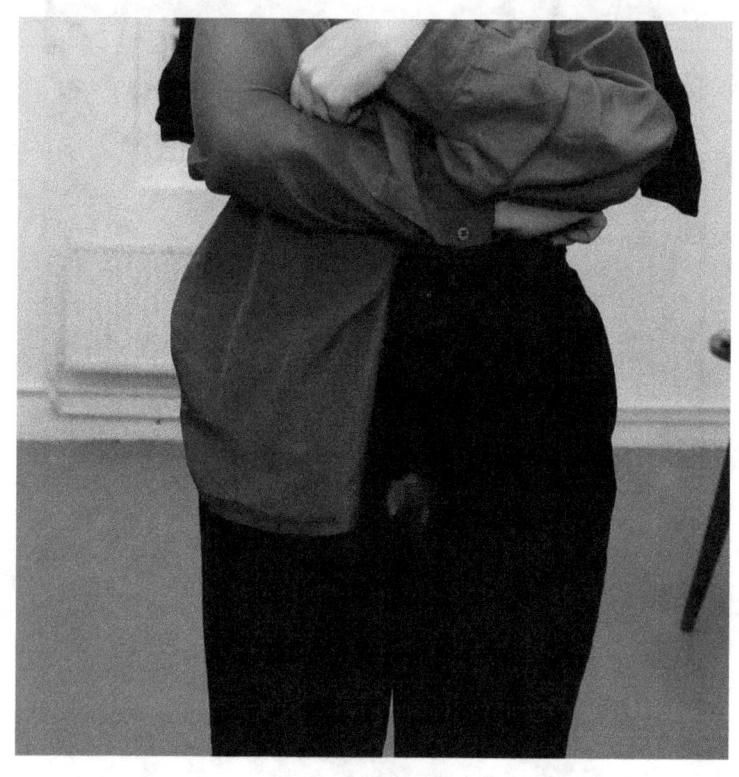

Yuying, Huang, (2023). Monthly, [photography
(performance documentation)]

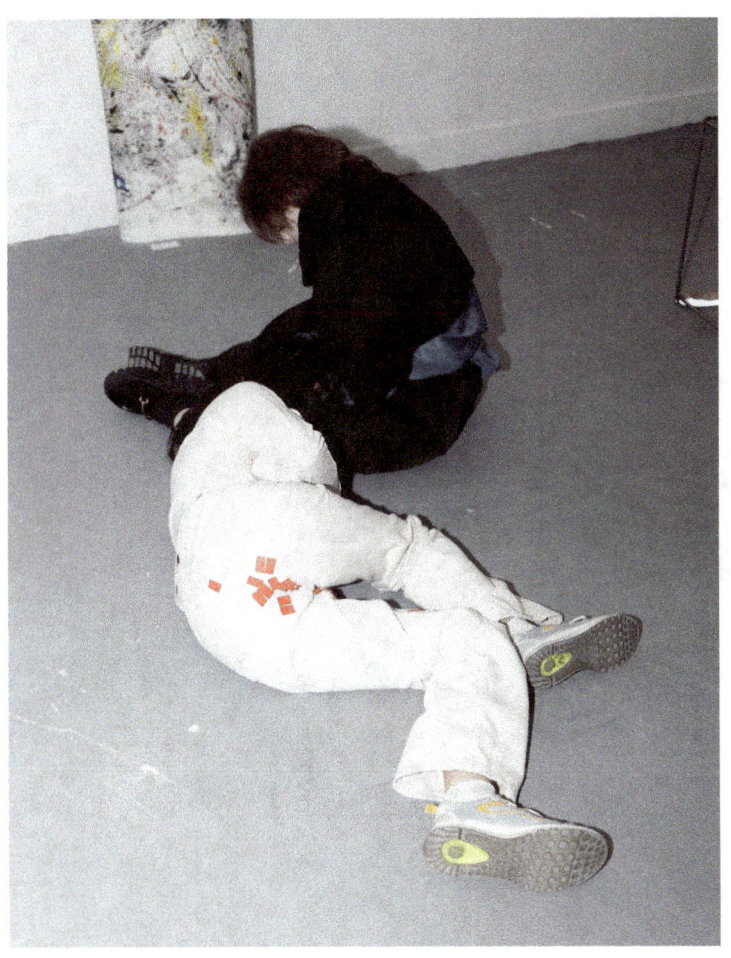

Yuying, Huang, (2023). Monthly, [photography
(performance documentation)]

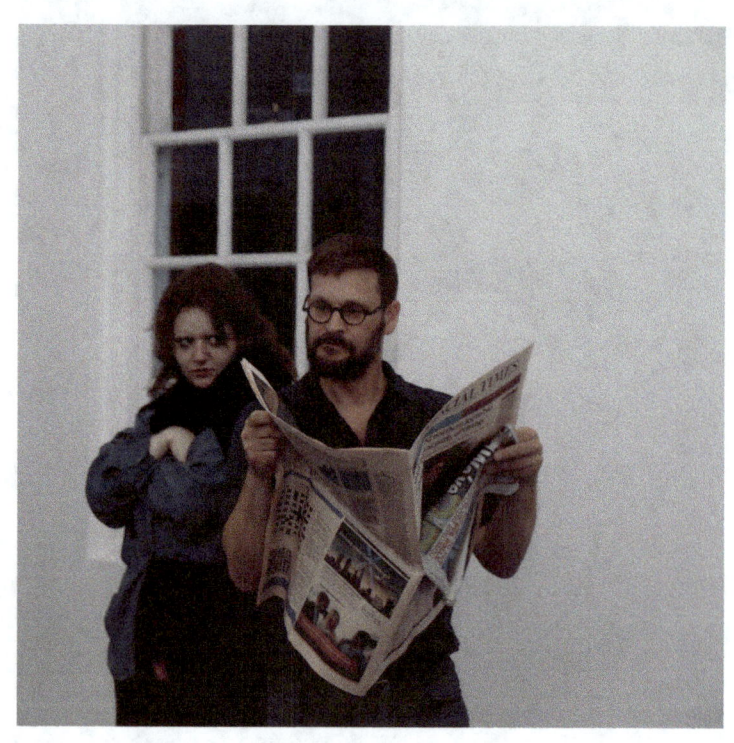

Yuying, Huang, (2023). Monthly, [photography (performance documentation)]

Yuying Huang (b.1998) is a performance and installation artist based in London and Shanghai. She holds an MA in Fine Art from Chelsea College of Arts and a BA in Public Art from China Academy of Art. Her work explores the concept of "image", seeking to understand daily life under the influence of the internet, often through the disarming effects of humor, and drawing from the theories of visual imagery and technology. Her pieces also addressing social issues through context-based artworks.

Equinox

F. Nadi

A poem is a dead thing,
My page a grave (a game)
Yard for the formless beings bound by words
Does it open me?
The hardness of this bodiliness
Into smaller solid stones
The headstone cracking
Tomb revealed
A beach of a thousand tiny bits
The only thing left to hold
I am left,
Standing on an island of bones
I am excreting what is
Left of me
Squeezing the solid and the these sweet somethings this
salt of the sea
Coffee grounds I am brown future of now
The teeth and tongue at the mouth
Of the beast

Equinox

Later, I can see it now, they will dig these words up,

With the ease, I can see it now,

You are unfolding me now,

Inch by inch,

Inheriting my pain

My heart

The pattern of your distress

The dum dum of the muscle in your breast

The way your bones formed from your cells

and the way you formed in her body the cell

Of the womb

The grotesque and penetrable and

the hollow that holds

The Calling-

inch by inch, we become

And as we realise, realised

We dying, died

Our fingers calcified

The confines of us immortalised

Perpetualised

Ossified

These words ossified

And terrorised

By our own fate we prophesise

Equinox

Our demise,
Playing by the rules of the skeletons we come out of to
find
Playing the game in that circle they ritualised,
Who wrote the ways you would weave yourself so
woefully.
Could you describe your death midflight?
Could you look your creator in the eye.
A poem is something flimsy
Worn for a night and closeted
Or closed in a bookshelf
Hidden in a hiding spot
Used in a back alley and deposited,
Could you use these words
to make love to the deadness of your eye
And the things between your thighs, and that thing
before we become other
Another line
Could you hold yourself im your grace grave
Could your bones amd blood imagine to live,
Imagine to forgive
Yourself for the tomb you were born from

Equinox

That you carry
Like A Calling
That you bear oceans from,
That you birth stones
And rough and tumble from
These clumsy words
Falling like bodies
(The fields of your falling
The lumps of your caress)
Could you call me in?
As we scream in the agony
of Burning Stars, of Becoming
Of betraying our bottomness
As our screams prescribe us in the endless silence
Broken, born by a poem of noise,

Could you read me backwards
To where it started
When we died.

F. Nadi is not an artist. They self-published their first chapbook in 2023, The Inside Out. Their works are experimental; karmic culminations of consciousness, realised through the 'author' as medium. Born in Cardiff, they currently reside in the cracks between Albion and Turkiye.

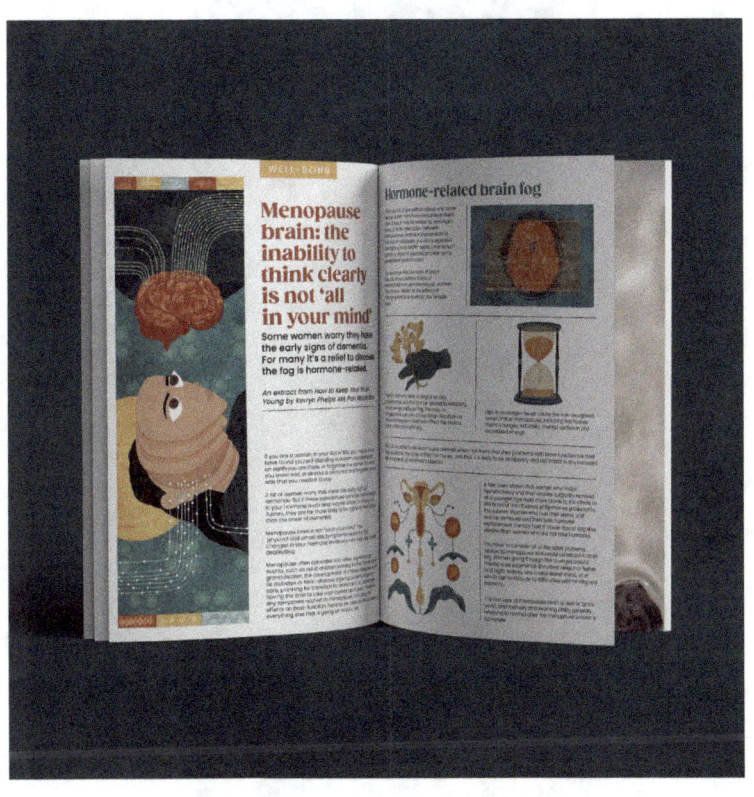

Srinivas, Vasundhara. (2024). Menopause brain, [Digital]

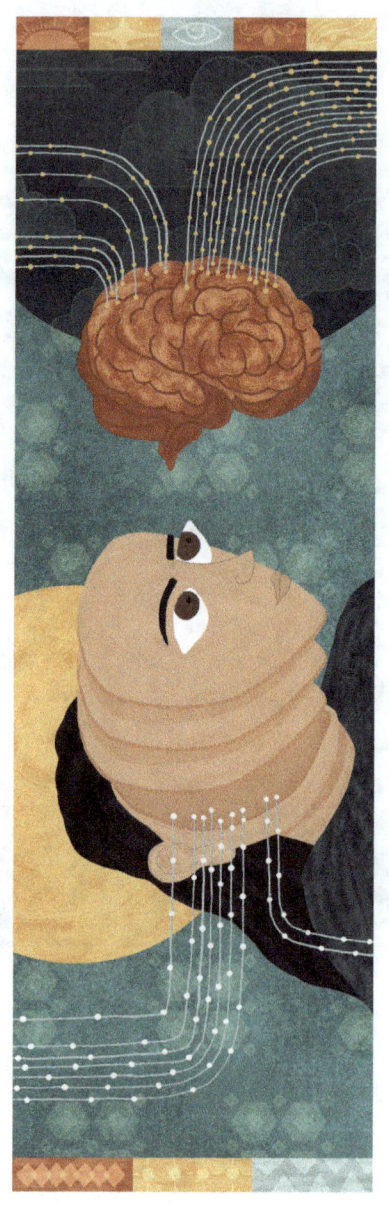

Srinivas, Vasundhara. (2024). Menopause
brain, [Digital]

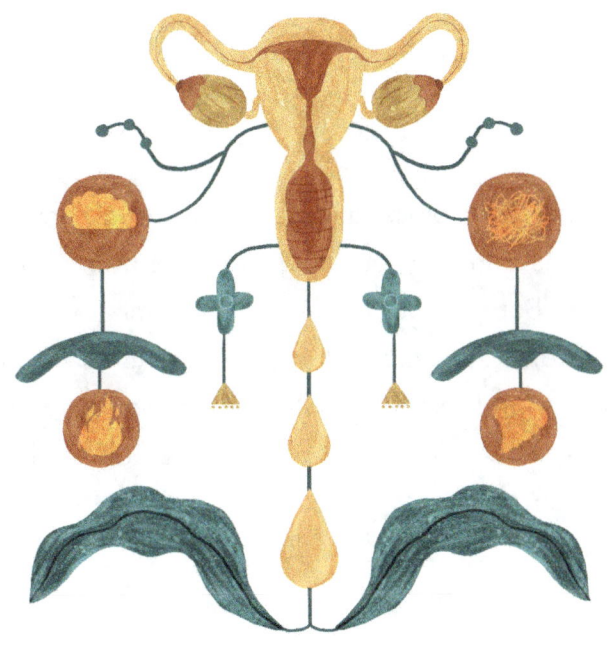

Srinivas, Vasundhara. (2024). Menopause
brain, [Digital]

Vasundhara Srinivas is a self-taught visual artist from India who is currently pursuing MA Illustration from Arts University Bournemouth. A striking mix of colors, detailing, and symbolism, her work seeks to challenge perceptions and evoke a sense of resonance. Her work mainly explores manifestations of mental health and visualizes emotions.

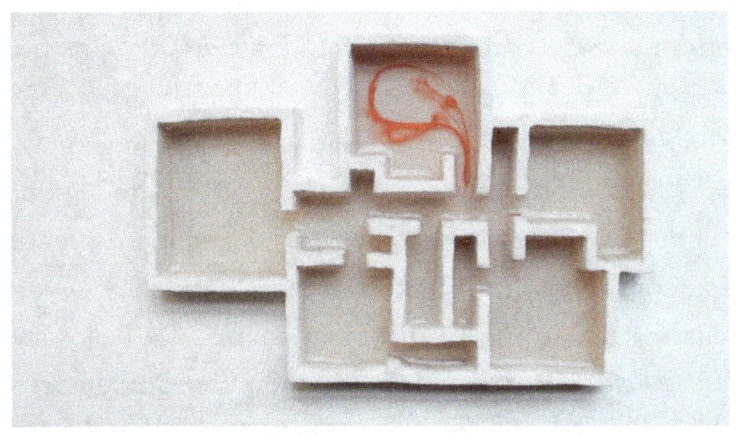

Wilschanski, Ye'ela. (2017).The Maze, [video,
8:48 minutes]

https://www.youtube.com/watch?
v=GFQhPoLiYhU

Ye'ela Wilschanski is an a interdisciplinary artist living and working in New York City. She has had solo performances and exhibitions at Parent Company Gallery, The Border Gallery, mhPROJECTnyc, Das Schaufenster, A.I.R. Gallery, and Movement Research at The Judson Church. Residencies include Monira Foundation Performance Residency ,Ponderosa Artist Residency and Lake Studio Dance Residency Awards include NYSCA/NYFA Artist Fellowship, LABA Fellowship, ILYSM Artist Grant, and Foundation for Contemporary Arts Emergency Grant. Wilschanski holds an MFA from Hunter College and a BFA from Bezalel Academy of Art and Design, including a student exchange program at the School of the Museum of Fine Arts, Boston.

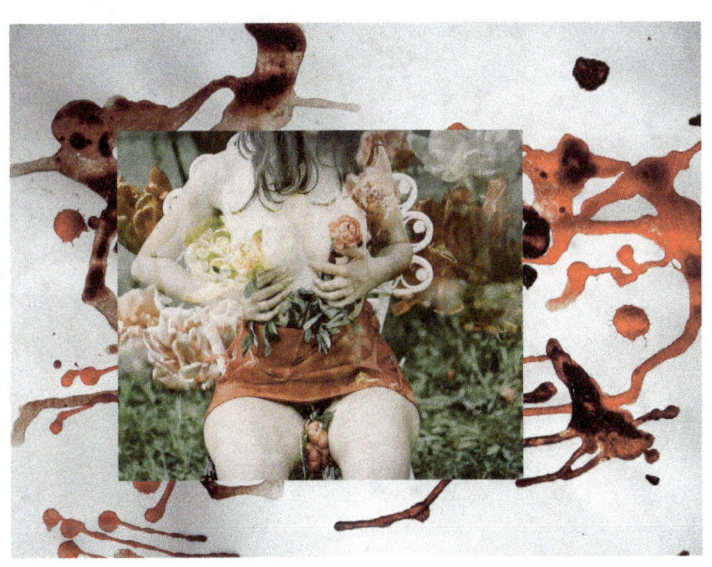

Laetitia Heisler, (2024). Breast PMS, [analog
photograph and menstrual blood].

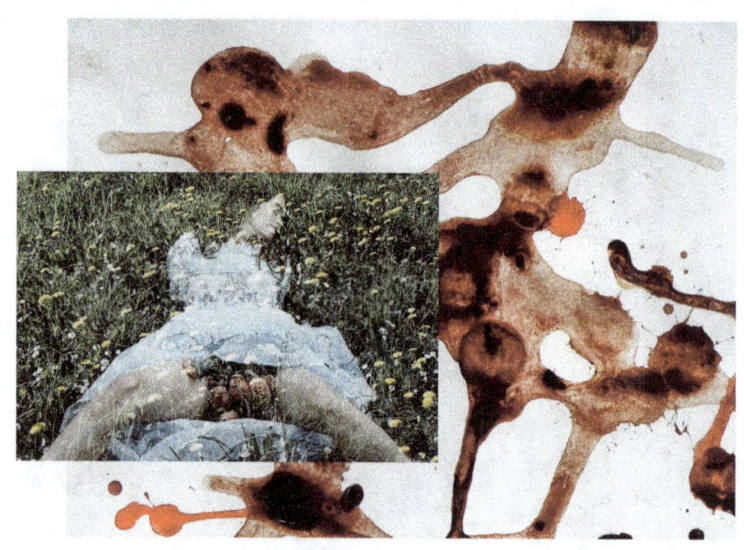

Laetitia Heisler, (2024). Cycles Invisibilisés,
[analog photograph and menstrual blood].

Laetitia Heisler, a French-German visual artist based in northern Germany, creates surrealistic visuals using old analog cameras and darkroom techniques, evoking "a sort of Alice in Wonderland world," as curator Anthony Fawcett described her work. Through photographic multiple exposures and extreme darkroom processes, Heisler pushes the boundaries of photography to produce visually stunning, psychedelic, and sometimes disturbing imagery.

Her work transcends beauty and perfection, aiming instead to capture the essence of human experience in both the natural and virtual worlds. By using self-portraiture, Heisler's photographs invite viewers to reflect on their relationship with femininity and humanity. She welcomes everyone into a realm where reality merges with imagination, imperfections intrigue, and emotions are exposed. Each image is an invitation to contemplation and introspection, challenging viewers to explore the depths of their own contradictions and existence.

a period of change

Freya Fu

I had always wanted to get my period. All of my friends had already gotten theirs, and even some girls from younger grades had as well. I was starting to think that maybe I was abnormal, that my body did not work the way it was supposed to.

Then it happened.

I remember sitting on the toilet seat and seeing a faint brown spot on my underwear, a signal that I had gotten my first period. To my surprise, rather than the life-changing experience I had anticipated, I was greeted by many rounds of stomachaches, mood swings, and food cravings. My body began to change with puberty, and for the first time in my life, I experienced period cramps. No one had warned me about these changes.

The truth is, that periods and menstrual hygiene are often topics that are rarely talked about, despite them being a natural cycle that most women go through. The brief sessions about menstruation in health class were often awkward and rushed, and many young girls are too embarrassed even to say the word out loud, often replacing the word "period" with "it." As the years passed, it became clear that while everyone knew about periods, no one talked about them openly. The social stigma regarding periods not only made them uncomfortable to talk about; it has become a toxin, restraining menstrual hygiene & affecting the lives of millions of girls across the globe.

a period of change

After doing more research on this issue, I found that almost 60% of women felt period shame and that as many as 500 million people do not have access to basic menstrual hygiene products. Determined to improve the status quo, I co-founded Vending4Change, a student-led nonprofit organization aimed at menstrual equity and period dignity. This past year, we delivered over 400 period products to shelters and raised over 700 dollars to fund menstrual hygiene kits. Our vision for this upcoming year is to continue spreading awareness about period poverty and host educational workshops on menstrual health at primary schools that lack the resources to do so.

Starting Vending4Change taught me that change begins with action. I had never thought that a high school student could create change on such a prominent social issue. However, I realized everyone can make an impact, big or small, regardless of age. By simply speaking up and educating ourselves, we can ensure that every person has the dignity and resources they deserve.

Periods are a natural part of our bodies. We shouldn't have to look around the classroom before checking our pants because we are too embarrassed about others seeing a leak. We shouldn't have to hide period products in our sleeves when walking to the bathroom, scared of what our peers would think of us. We should be able to state our needs and discuss periods with dignity, free of judgment and taboo. For this to happen, we must all do our part in breaking the silence.

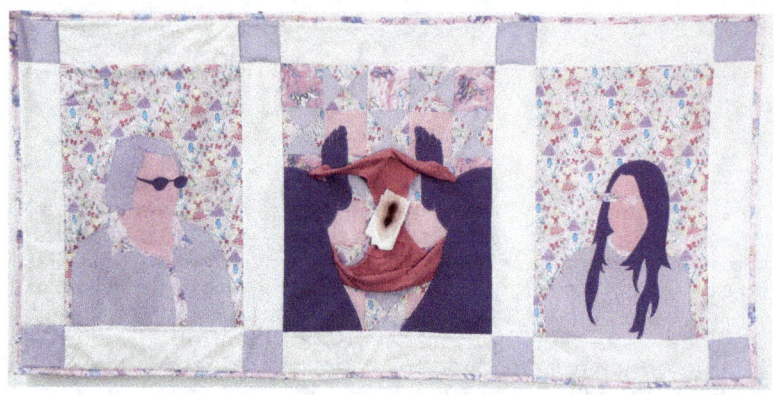

Sneed, Izzy. (2022). ToiletPaperPeriod,
[quilted cotton fabric, applique, underwear]

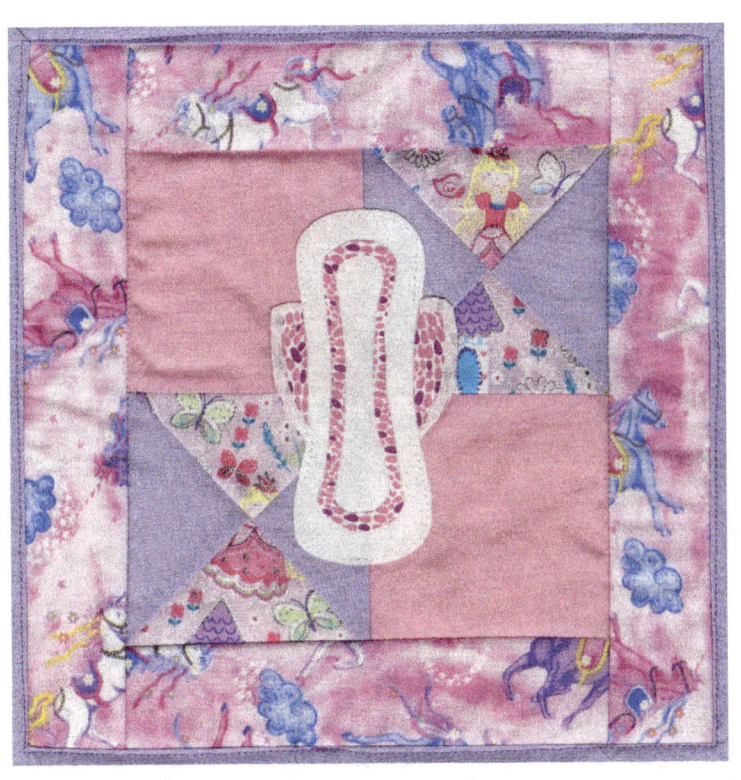

Sneed, Izzy. (2022). But I'm Only 10!, [quilted cotton fabric, applique].

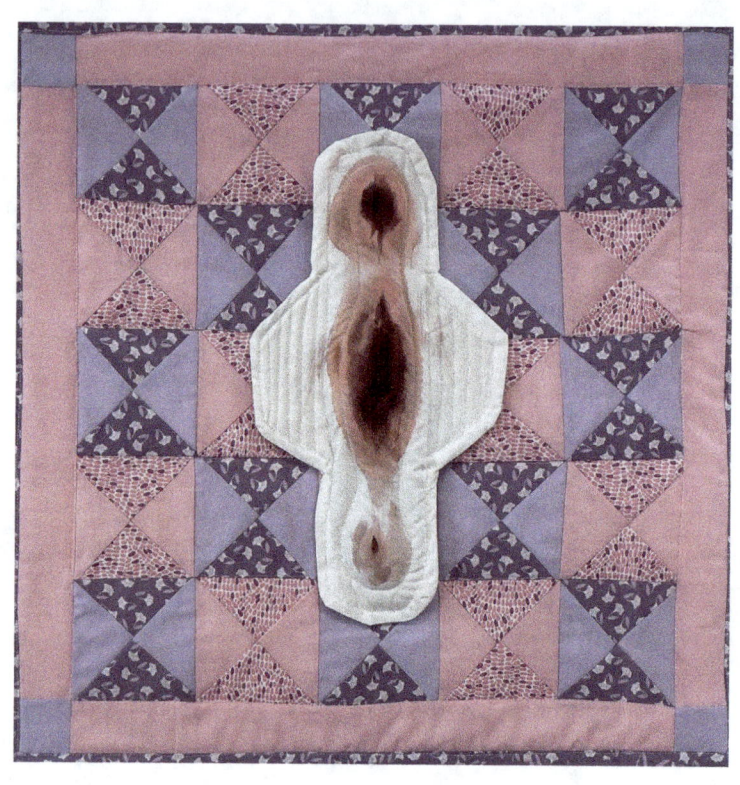

Sneed, Izzy. (2022). Pad, [quilted cotton fabric, applique].

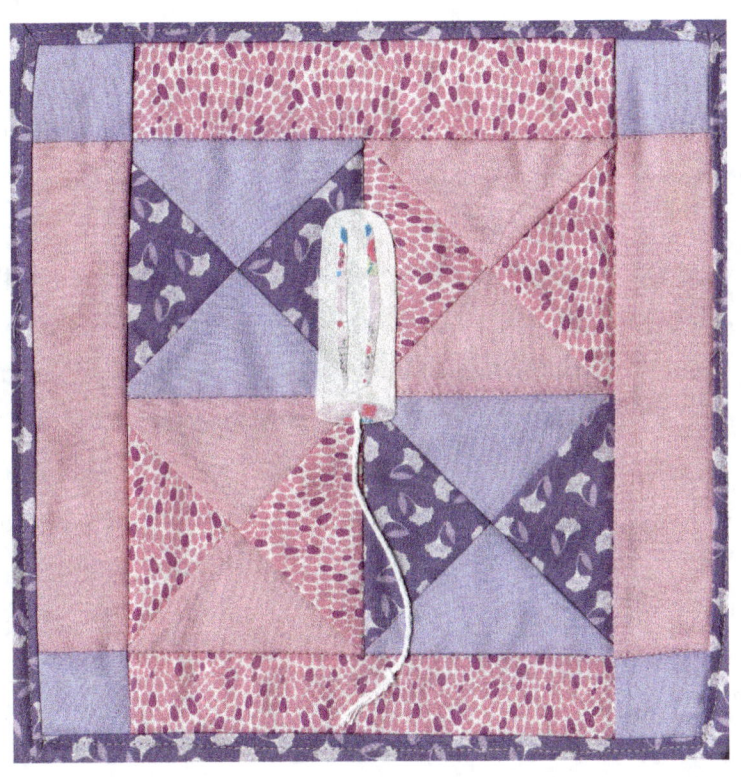

Sneed, Izzy. (2022). I am a Woman!, [quilted
cotton fabric, applique].

Izzy Sneed was raised in the rural town of Preston, Missouri. Her family's complicated and frequent relocations throughout her life has significantly influenced her artistic practice. Currently, she lives with her partner and cat in the North Dallas metroplex. Sneed graduated in 2024 with a Masters in Fine Arts at Texas Woman's University in Denton, TX. She has participated in many juried exhibitions, including the John Weinkein exhibition juried by Vicki Meek and Represent: Misapprehended juried by Enrique Cervantes. Furthermore, Sneed has been honored with several awards, notably receiving an honorable mention in the UNT Libraries' 13th Biennial Artists' Book Competition for her work.

athletes and their menstruation experience

With Red & Period Museum

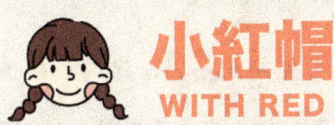 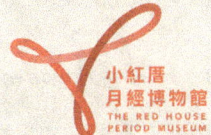

For athletes assigned female at birth, menstruation is inseparable from their status on the field and in their daily training. Five athletes were interviewed on stories regarding menstruation, with their experiences encompassing various similarities and differences.

We interviewed five athletes, including gymnasts, track and field athletes, rowers, lifeguards, and amateur free divers. Through one-on-one interviews with people who have been in the sports field for a long time, we learned things that the public may not have known or noticed in the past, with the hope that others who love sports can become more comfortable with menstruation and their bodies.

Even if you have menstrual pain, you have to tolerate it.

Many people have experienced menstrual pain. Usually, we may choose to sit or lie down to rest. So, as an athlete who coaches or competes, what should you do when you encounter menstrual pain?

According to this interview, we found that even if most athletes experience menstrual pain during work or practice, they will still grit their teeth and try to hold on. Unless they are extremely uncomfortable, they will not take a break or ask the coach for menstrual leave. This has a lot to do with the content and nature of the athletes' work. Competitive athletes need to maintain and improve their ability through consistent practice, and cannot risk taking time off from training as it may negatively impact their performance.

"Our training is interrupted by menstruation, which will have a great impact on the effectiveness of our regiment. But boys don't have this problem." - Xiaowen (middle-distance running)

"I hope that the children who come to the swimming class make progress, so I don't take my own physical condition into account. I just coach the way I usually do, but I will feel extremely tired after the class." - Arun (swimming)

Inappropriate menstrual products cause skin injuries

Ranging from tampons to pads and menstrual cups, people may choose to try a variety of modern menstrual products. However, whether or not athletes have the corresponding resources and education to understand the pros and cons of various products and choose the products that are most suitable for them, will affect their physical state and performance.

Gymnast Jiarong said that she often worries about exposed sanitary pads when wearing a tight-fitting leotard; free diver Anna and swimming coach Arun must use tampons because they engage in water sports; and rower Yiting and middle-distance runner Xiaowen also shared that during exercise, the constant movement of their legs and friction against their sanitary pads can easily lead to skin ruptures, which causes unbearable pain.

"If you get the 'wings' all the way to the edge of the sanitary napkin, they will rub and break the skin. It hurts, it really hurts!" - Yiting (rowing)

Menstrual blood leakage is difficult to deal with. When athletes exercise, they often need to swing their bodies and change positions frequently. Regardless of whether they have used menstrual products or not, menstrual blood leakage often occurs.

In the sports field, it is difficult to get away with dealing with menstrual blood while working and competing. They can only endure it for a while, wait until after work or the game is over, and then rush to the toilet to change menstrual products.

"My period came suddenly halfway through exercise. The amount wasn't a lot, but it kind of seeped outside my gym attire. I didn't have time to put a (sanitary pad) on at the time." - Jiarong (gymnastics)

"I just felt wet down there, I didn't think much about it." - Anna (free diving)

Athletes' confessions:

"It's just described by the word 'trouble'." - Arun (swimming)

"As soon as my period comes, I feel better." - Anna (freediving)

"Hmm... it means I'm still young, so I love and hate it at the same time." - Yiting (rowing)

"The existence of a period is really like a person, with ups and downs." - Xiaowen (middle-distance running)

"I find it very troublesome because I have menstrual pain. Every time the pain is so severe, I want to remove my uterus." - Jiarong (gymnastics)

We conducted interviews with athletes who were engaged in five sports: gymnastics, free diving, middle-distance running, swimming, and rowing. We started from their perspectives and sorted out their past experiences through narratives.

Here, I would like to express my special thanks to Jiarong, Anna, Xiaowen, Arun, and Yiting for their willingness to enthusiastically share their stories with readers, so that people with similar experiences can feel that they are not alone. Through observation and recognition, you can feel the connection and intimacy between yourself and your body, be aware of every texture and every aching pain, face up to the physiological conditions that you may have never thought about or paid attention to, and learn to deal with them. When we coexist with and understand menstruation, we also accept our own bodies.

Menstruation is closely related to each of our lives. We have seen that athletes may encounter challenges on the sports field due to their biological sex or the physiological phenomenon of menstruation. Among them, there are many common and similar experiences, yet there are also unique situations that are very different from each other. Therefore, we understand that everyone is different, and through collective stories, highlight each experience. Regarding menstruation and the body, there is no good or bad. There is only advocacy through sharing, dialogue, and understanding. This is also the tenderness that [Menstruation in the Workplace] wants to bring to readers. We look forward to exploring and pondering together with everyone.

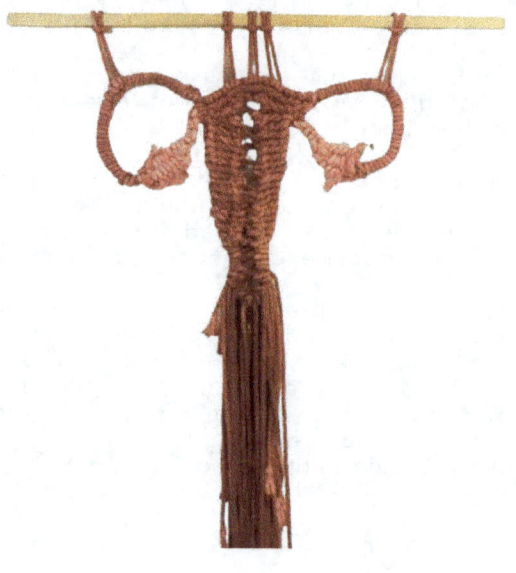

Virok, Eszter Tunde. (2024). Period Falls,
[macrame]

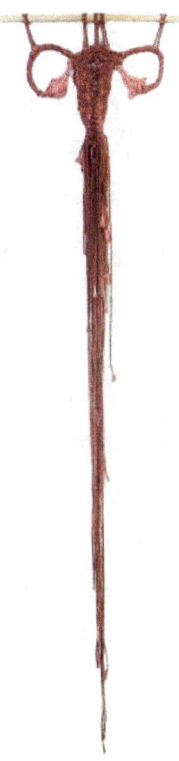

Virok, Eszter Tunde. (2024). Period Falls,
[macrame]

Virok originally finished her higher education in puppet acting, but was always drawn to visuality and visual storytelling. In the last year, she rediscovered herself in visual arts, and in its versatility. She started to learn more about different techniques, creating works connected to local cultures and issues.

Virok's background in puppet theater allows her to think more openly in using different materials, to get connected with them more deeply, and to include a personal narrative behind her works. She collects stories from people, creates pieces from the viewpoints and experiences of other creatures, and relives others lives and narratives. Visual arts feels like kind of a theatre for her in that sense.

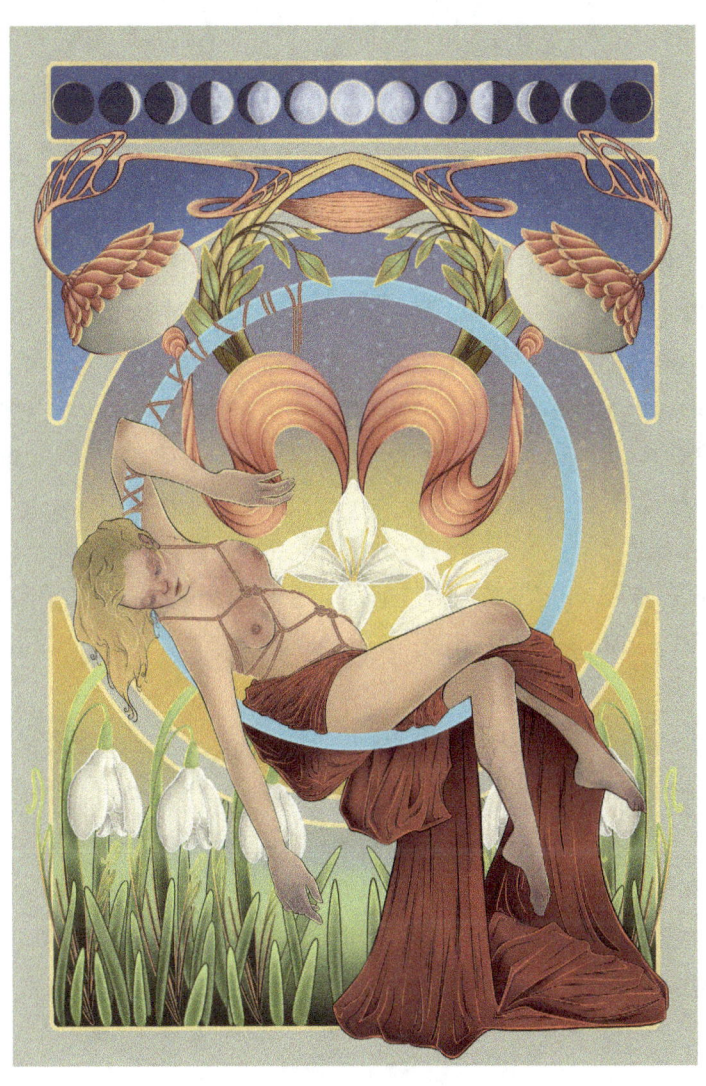

Elizabeth, Aubry (2023) Loss, [Digital]

Every person with a uterus will fall on the spectrum of failing hormones. Whether the odds are impossible for a viable birth, a miscarriage, unending vaginally bleeding, disregard while postpartum, seemingly eternal exhaustion. Every aspect of our bodies are challenged on a day to day basis, even for women who "have it all figured out" according to their peers. The loss of autonomy, and identity, are on a 28 day cycle, with 365 days of bleeding in the meantime.

Elizabeth has been dealing with a multitude of reproductive and hormone "phenomena" and after a particularly traumatizing miscarriage, this painting just, came to be. Her goal as an artist is to help people process the harder things in life and she figured she should do some of that reflecting too.

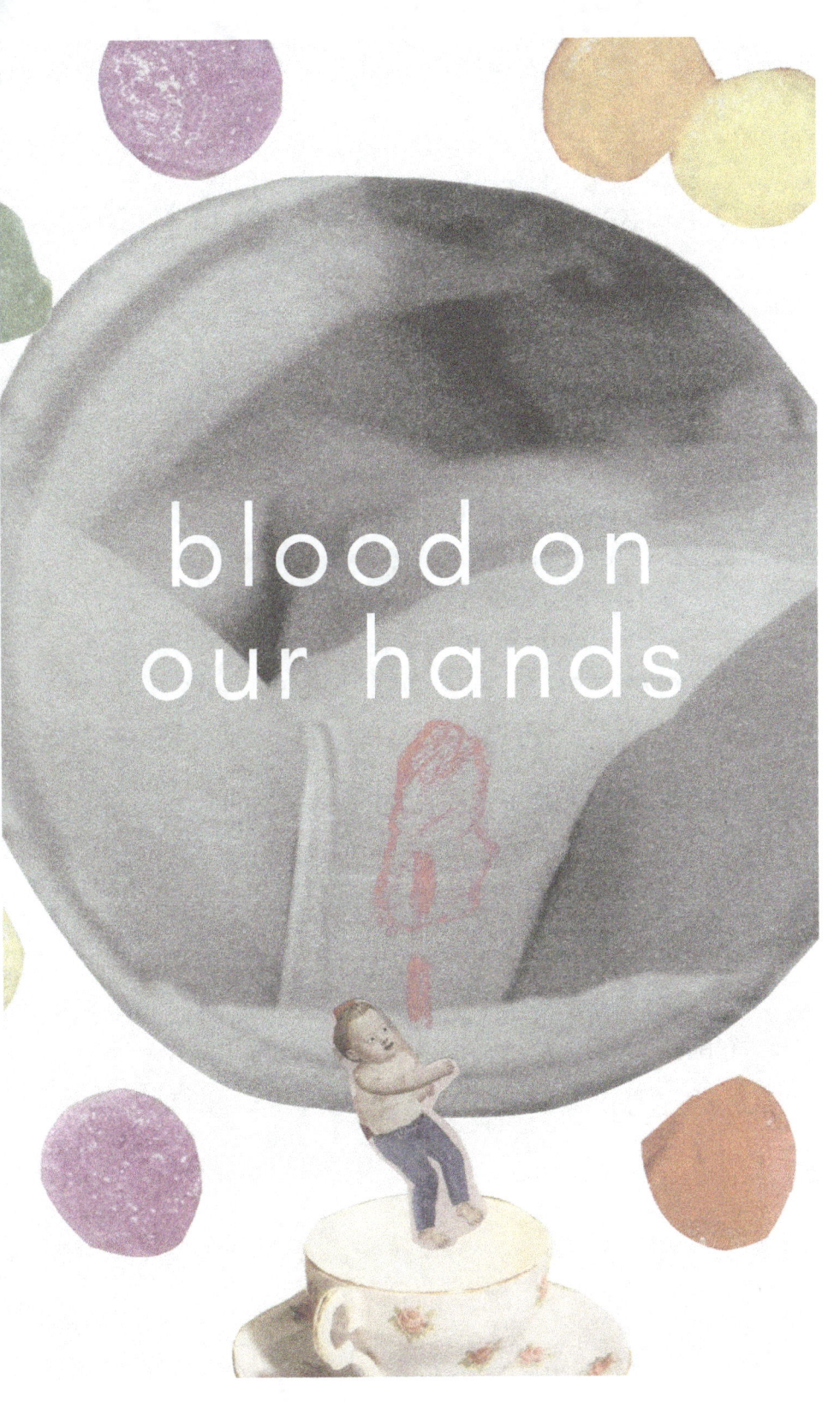

blood on our hands

"blood on our hands" platforms artworks that boldly confront issues of bodily autonomy, menstrual equality, and female rage.

These pieces challenge societal norms and systemic barriers that hinder access to menstrual products, healthcare, and education. They amplify voices demanding justice and recognition, urging a reclamation of autonomy over one's body and experiences.

Despite the frustration surrounding failing systems, these pieces exude empowerment, a testament to the ability for art to inspire hope and drive solutions to health inequities.

Through vivid imagery and provocative symbolism, these artists ignite conversations on empowerment, resilience, and the pursuit of menstrual and gender equality via an intersectional lens.

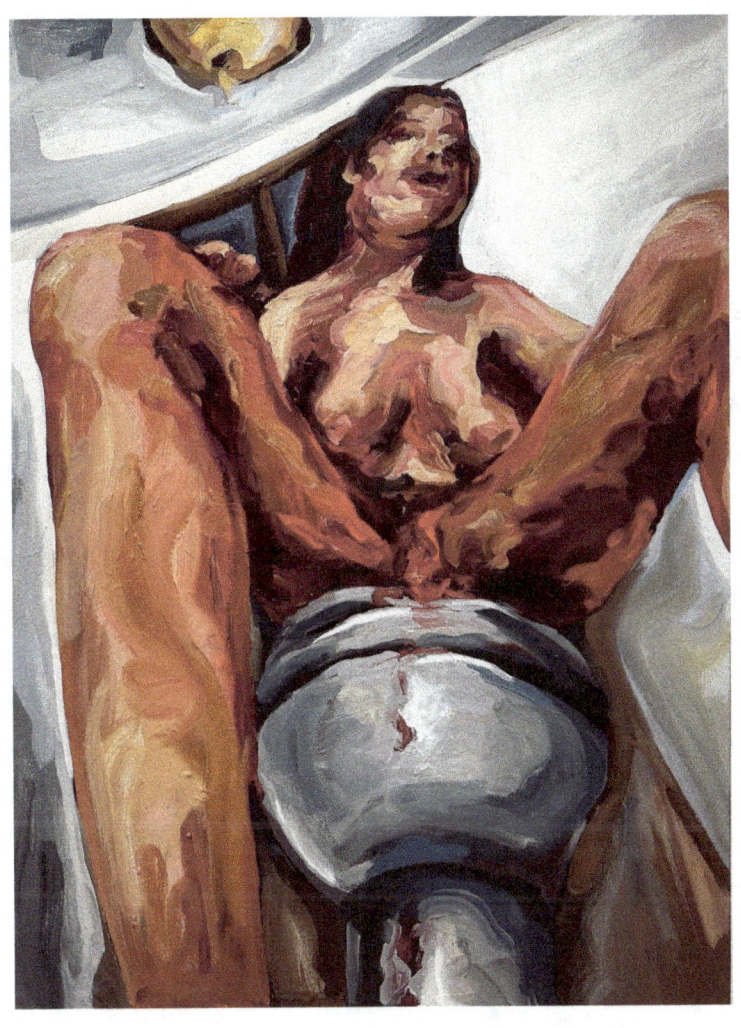

Covert, Isabella. (2024). Dripped, [Oil on canvas]

Isabella Covert is a painter born in Milwaukee, Wisconsin. She received a BFA from the University of Wisconsin-Madison in 2023 and is currently a MFA candidate and Graduate Fellowship recipient at the Savannah College of Art and Design. Covert's paintings comment on the mental complexities women experience due to the state of women's rights and reproductive rights in America, and the internal sensibility of feeling inside oneself. She has shown in group exhibitions both virtually and in person in galleries across the US including Chicago, Illinois, Laguna Beach, California, Cincinnati, Ohio, and New York. Covert currently lives and works in Savannah, GA.

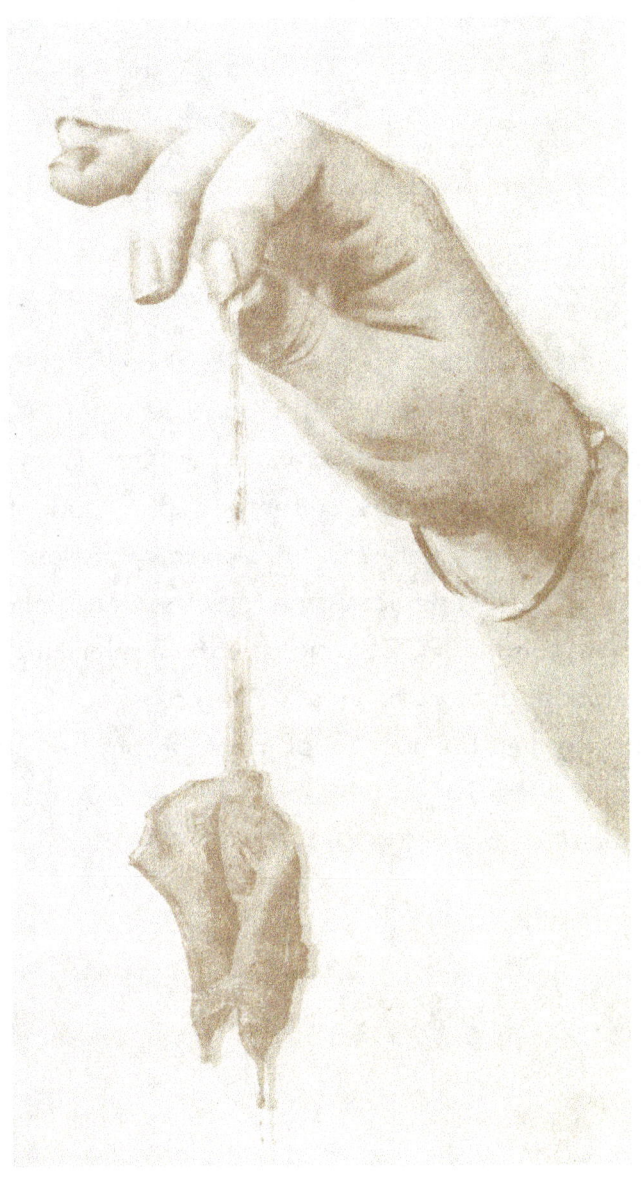

Glass, Kate. (2023). Untitled (Tampon),
[Menstrual blood gum bichromate print].

Kate Glass is a photographer and artist based in Lincoln, Nebraska. She received her Associate of Applied Science in Photography from Metropolitan Community College in 2023 and is currently a BFA student with emphasis in photography at the University of Nebraska - Lincoln. Glass's work focuses on topics such as polycystic ovarian syndrome (PCOS), menstruation, femininity, self-acceptance, and womanhood. She has special interest in pushing the boundaries of photography by playing with mixed media and bright colors in contrast with intense, taboo subject matter.

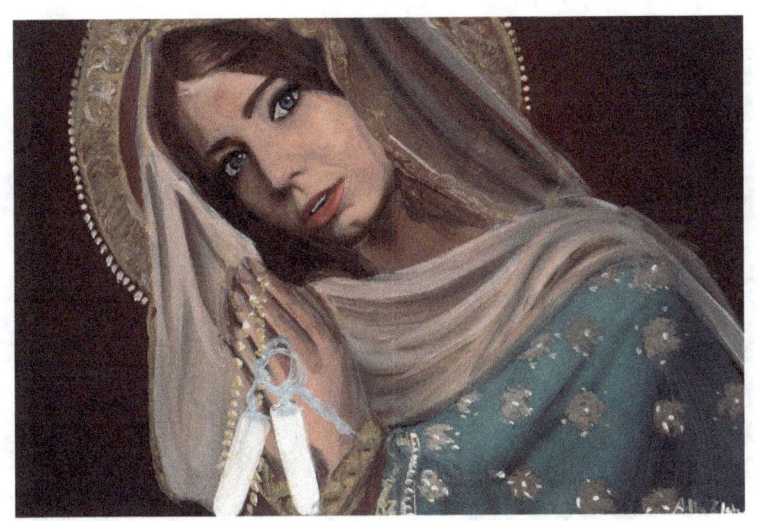

Zlatar, Ally. (2023) The Holy Period, [Acrylic]

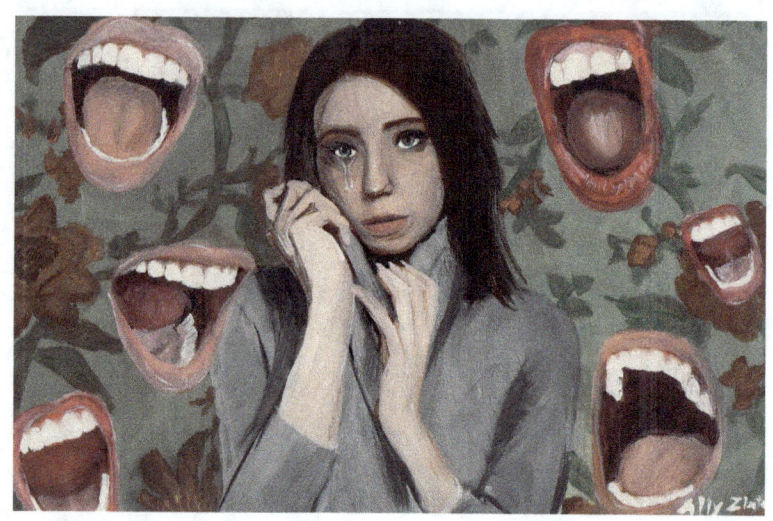

Zlatar, Ally. (2023) Voices Behind Bodies, [Acrylic]

Ally Zlatar is an artist, scholar and activist. She holds a BFA in Visual Art & Art History from Queen's University & an MLitt Curatorial Practice and Contemporary Art from the Glasgow School of Art. Her Doctorate of Creative Arts is with the University of Southern Queensland focusing on embodied experiences of mental illness in contemporary art. Zlatar is a Lecturer at the University of Glasgow and has taught at Glasgow International College, KICL London, and the University of Essex (UEIC).Her "This Body of Mine" campaign explores migrant experiences through creative voices and has helped support individuals and artists from refugee-seeking backgrounds globally. Ally Zlatar has received the highest accolade a young person can achieve for their humanitarian work; such as the Commonwealth Innovation Awards (2023), winner of The Princess Diana Legacy Award (2021), King Hamad Award for Youth Empowerment (2022), the Lieutenant Governor's Community Volunteer Award from the Ontario Government of Canada (2023) and also special recognition from The British Citizen Award (2022).

A period can be a gift to some and a curse to others. We must deeply understand the diverse experiences of periods in order to achieve true equity.

Ally Zlatar

Endometriosis: A Nightmare

A nightmare ravaging my insides

Stealing light and haunting life

Broken and fracturing what was once whole

A darkness swirling and mocking

Twisting tissue and bending the soul

Claiming all I had and can no longer hold

An unforgiving force of despair

Plucking at strings and untying sanity

Hidden pain that few understand or believe

Alexandra Low is a labor and delivery nurse, student Nurse Midwife/WHNP, and author. Her own journey with endometriosis has shaped numerous aspects of her life, namely her nursing and writing careers. For Alexandra, writing is a form of self-expression that has allowed her to process the grappling pain this disease has caused, as well as advocate for awareness. One of her hopes is that, in her lifetime, she sees the 10-year diagnosis delay drastically decrease and that pain is believed. This past year, she wrote an article reflecting on her experience living with endometriosis and the battle to obtain her diagnosis for The National Association of Nurse Practitioners in Women's Health's online journal. Additionally, her debut novel, "Losing My Skin," is a fantasy retelling of traditional selkie folklore with underlying threads of women's chronic pain woven throughout.

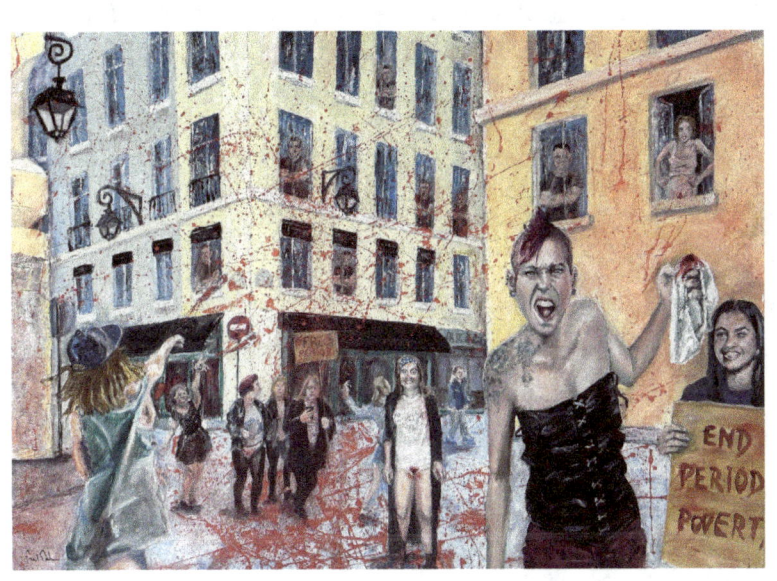

Fabre, Fred. (2019). Rouge, [oil]

Key highlights include participation in: (5th Base, London 2014), film installation (YALE University/Kensington Palace 2017), Modern Panic X (Guerrilla Zoo, London 2019), inclusion in academic discourse such as "Climate Action and Visual Culture" (University of Huddersfield, 2021), "Action Against Hate" (University of Westminster/Get the Trolls Out, 2023), and selected to exhibit in the Herbert Art Gallery and Museum (Coventry 2023).

Fred has also exhibited in shows in London, Athens, Prague, Budapest and Mexico. In November 2023, Fabre was granted the DYCP (Developing Your Creative Practice) award by Arts Council England. Fred is currently collaborating with The Wrong Gallery in Birmingham to develop a series of exhibitions. Awards include the Refresh Art Award (winner Our Times) in 2019, BAFTA winner in 2005 and a 2006 nomination for his camera work on documentaries.

Education: MFA – Chelsea College of Art 2006

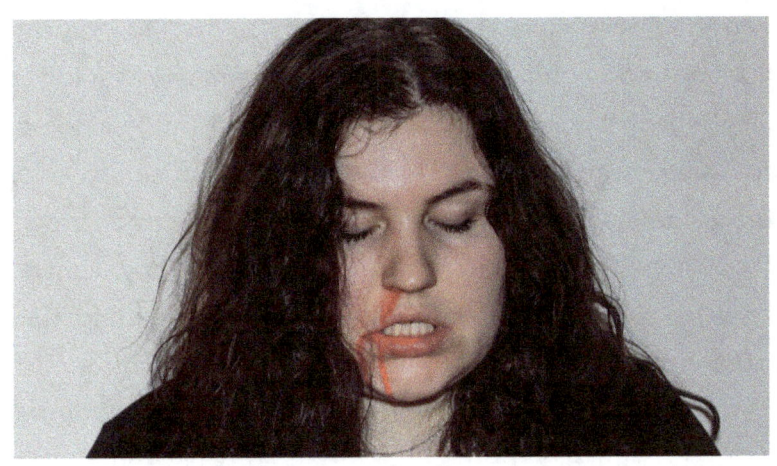

Smith, Daisy-Drew. (2023). Nosebleed,
[Gloss Print]

Daisy-Drew Smith works with photography and film, their current work uses photographic prints to create juxtapositions and references to horror movies. Smith is inspired by the surrealist aspects of this kind of cinema, focusing on the dream-like and heightened reality. They are interested in the parallels that stylised horror draws from real events and the effects of trauma. They want to keep true to 'movie magic', using editing, lighting and practical effects to create realistic scenes of horror. This film is inspired by the found footage genre and explores imagery with elevated sound, to create unseen horror. Smith uses their photos to create fake cinematic universes, they think of their various photo series as different films.

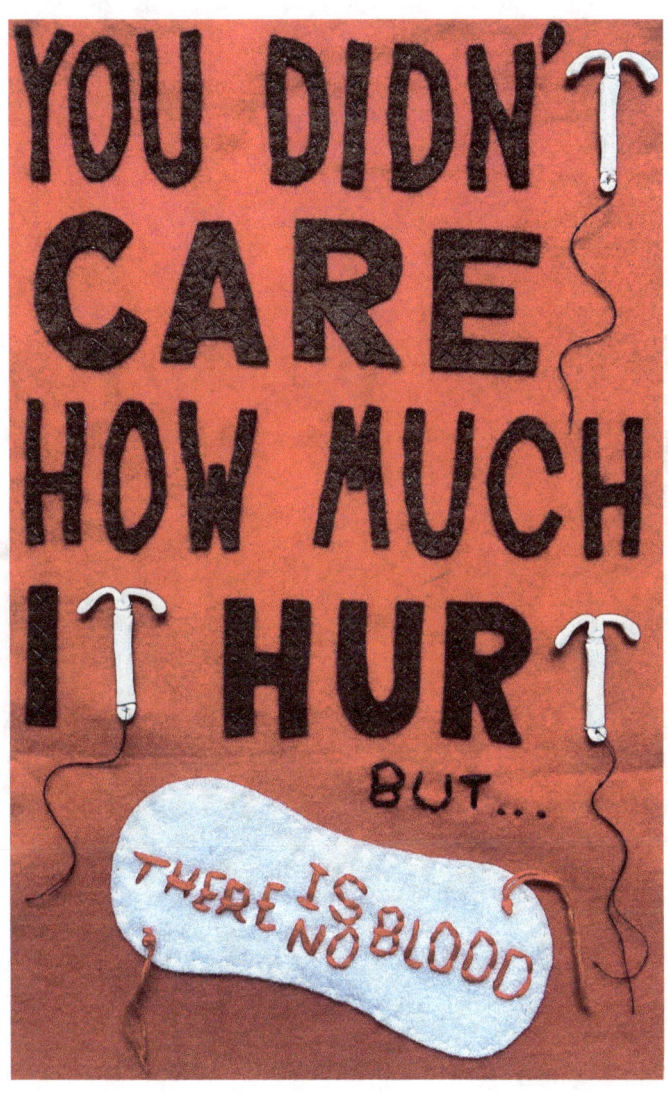

Kay, Madeleina. (2024). You Didn't Care,
[mixed media].

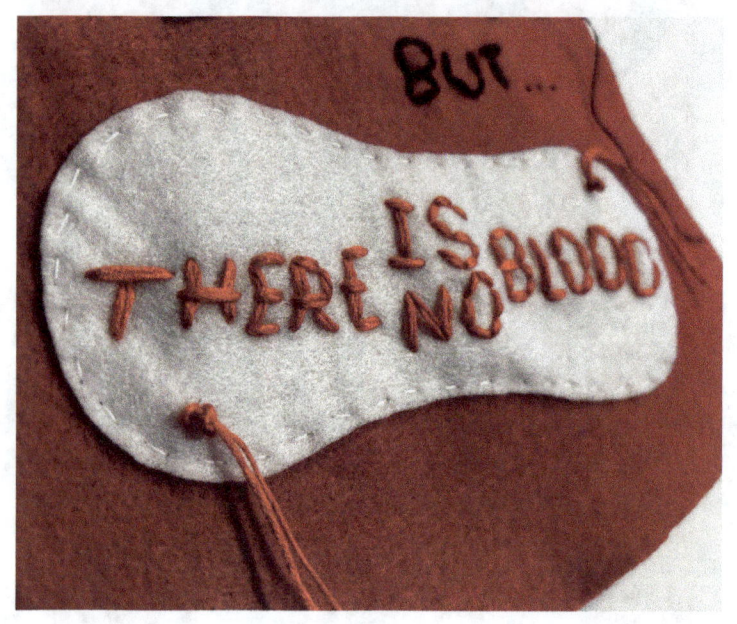

Kay, Madeleina. (2024). You Didn't Care (Detail), [mixed media].

Madeleina Kay is an artist and activist, awarded 'Young European of the year' (2018) - currently studying MA Fine Art at Central Saint Martins. She has written, illustrated and self-published nine books and contributed writing to the German National Library's 'House of Europe' book (2020), 'The Other Side: An Emotional Map of Britain' by GraphicDesign& (2020) and 'Ways of Protest', by Round Lemon' (2020). She has written and performed protest songs at events across Europe, including 'The Right to Vote' exhibition opening at the National Justice Museum, UK (2018), Glastonbury Festival, UK (2019), Aachen Town Hall (2022) and the European Parliament (2023). In 2019, she was awarded a 'Democracy Needs Imagination' grant from the European Cultural Foundation to deliver her project 'The Future is Europe', which was awarded the Charlemagne Youth Prize in 2020.

Menstrual stories from frontline medical staff

With Red & Period Museum

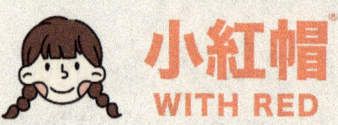 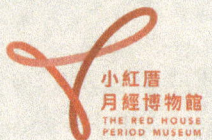

Seventy percent of medical staff in Taiwan are assigned female at birth. How does menstruation affect their lives? This time, With Red went to the frontlines of medical care and listened to the stories of medical staff.

During the COVID-19 pandemic, With Red received many letters from medical staff, saying that they had encountered many difficulties with menstruation.

What are the troubles and challenges faced on the frontline of medical care?
Can medical staff really take menstrual leave if they are menstruating while on duty?
In what ways can we ensure that the menstrual rights of medical staff are also protected?

In the past two months, partners of the With Red academic research team conducted in-depth interviews with six medical staff from different regions, work positions, and ages. They found that many medical staff shared common problems at work, including menstrual experiences.

Long Working Hours and Inability to Replace Menstrual Products

During the interviews, all medical staff repeatedly stressed that the nature of their work involves "long hours on duty" and that it is almost impossible to frequently change sanitary products.

"Because I really don't have time to change menstrual products," Cai Lin, a medical staff member, said. "I can only let it [menstrual blood] flow as hard as possible." This results in letting the menstrual blood leak and flow until she gets off work before changing her pants.

More than half of the medical staff interviewed also mentioned that "when on duty, they usually use night-time, multi-volume sanitary napkins, or even diapers, and wear them for a long time. This way, they only need to use one piece a day and do not need to change them all the time, which can avoid any possible clashing with their workload."

However, this was an abnormal way to use sanitary napkins, and that this often made them worry about menstrual blood leakage while working, and that they would have to work like that all day long.

Some medical staff mentioned that they have tried other more comfortable, reusable, and multi-type menstrual products during their work, such as menstrual underwear, which can absorb menstrual blood for a long time and is more breathable. Some people also mentioned that they use tampons that can be left in the body for a longer period of time, but Yijun mentioned that "I have tried using them, but I am not used to it yet." Or they have already used tampons and still have no time to change them after they are full of menstrual blood. As such, there remains concern about leakage.

Hot, Uncomfortable Protective Clothing Causing Redness, Swelling, and Rashes

Staying at their posts for long periods of time without breaks, coupled with the need to wear sweltering protective clothing that is difficult to put on and take off during the COVID-19 pandemic, have made the menstrual problems faced by medical staff even more severe during the pandemic.

When changing menstrual products, medical staff need to remove all protective equipment. However, it takes about 5 to 10 minutes to put on and take off protective clothing, masks, gloves, and shoe covers. Because they need to work continuously, most people can only take a break at noon. During the day, it is almost impossible to change frequently.

During the pandemic, due to concerns about the risk of transmission caused by central air-conditioning, air-conditioning was not allowed in some wards. Medical staff were already sweating profusely under their protective clothing. During menstruation, medical staff who are accustomed to using night-use, multi-volume sanitary napkins, or pants-type sanitary napkins while on duty cannot avoid staying in a hot and uncomfortable environment for a long time, which may lead to skin rashes, backache, and lower abdominal pain.

No Time to Go to the Toilet, Fear of Drinking Water, High Risk of Infection

Because of the long hours on duty, the inability to predict when patients will appear, the inability to estimate the number of patients, and the special nature of their work, medical staff are unable to go to the toilet at any time while on duty, even if they risk increased infection. During work, they still often dare not drink water and often hold their urine.

"And even if you want to go to the toilet, the time may not be suitable," medical staff Yong Xin mentions. She states that they often have to rush to the toilet when patients are entering and exiting the clinic, or when they know that a certain patient will have a long interview. Therefore, many colleagues around her have experience with urinary tract infections.

High-Pressure Work and Shifts Affect Menstruation

Being in an extremely high-pressure working environment for a long time, coupled with the nature of the shift system, some medical staff who work night shifts often suffer from problems such as irregular and painful menstrual cycles.

Medical staff Cai Lin also mentioned, "As long as I know my period is coming that day, no matter if there is pain or not, I will take painkillers early in the morning because I am afraid it will affect my work." She continued, "Sometimes menstruation will cause pain. I may really want to vomit, but I have to cope with the high-pressure and fast pace, so taking preventive painkillers has become a must."

Menstrual Leave that is available but Hard to Take

"No one has asked for [menstrual leave] so far." Almost all medical staff mentioned this in interviews.

"Everyone will hold on at work. Even if they vomit during menstruation, they won't ask for help," medical staff Mei Shu said helplessly. Their considerations are mostly due to the fact that each person is familiar with and responsible for different types of work, the fact that the hospital is short of manpower, and that the shifts are all scheduled. If they ask for leave, they are worried that no one can replace them, and that it will cause trouble for their colleagues. Therefore, even if they feel unwell due to menstruation, they don't take menstrual leave.

Another consideration is that most people don't know the rules regarding requests for menstrual leave, and they are more afraid of affecting their performance appraisals, or their supervisor's impression of them. "On the surface, it seems that you can ask for leave, but privately no one dares to ask for it." Yujie said in the interview. Therefore, menstrual leave has become a visible but hard-to-reach existence in the daily work of medical staff.

Sanitary Products Are Not Provided in the Workplace and Are Difficult to Obtain

In the medical field, difficulty in obtaining sanitary products is also a major problem.
"Many times if we don't have sanitary products on hand, we have to cover them with toilet paper or borrow them from colleagues in an emergency," said Xiao Qi, a medical staff member. Another medical worker, Cai Lin, also mentioned, "When menstruation occurs suddenly at work, the place where menstrual products are placed or purchased is usually a little far away from the workplace. Even if there is a break, there is no time to get them, so I can only drink water."

Because the place where medical staff keep their menstrual products and the place where they work are often in different locations (for example, the menstrual products are placed in lockers, but they need to stay in the clinic, intensive care unit, nursing station, front desk, etc. for a long time when they are on duty), it becomes an impossible task to get the menstrual products first and then run to the toilet to change them during the very tight and sometimes almost non-existent break time.

Being quarantined due to the COVID-19 pandemic, or finding that you don't have menstrual products with you in a busy situation, and having to leave work to obtain sanitary products are challenges that many medical staff have mentioned.

"Take care of your discomfort quickly so you can take care of the patient," Yijun said at the end of the interview.
This is a common sentiment and daily struggle mentioned by the medical staff interviewed. Those on the front line always put others first, even if it means ignoring their own physiological needs.

At the end of the interview, medical staff Cai Lin also told With Red: "Most of my colleagues in the unit are women, and will definitely encounter menstrual problems. I am very happy that someone can speak for us, because I would like others to understand my experience when menstruating. Usually, in the workplace, people who don't menstruate or who don't feel uncomfortable during menstruation may wonder why I am so slow and inefficient today, or why I look so ugly."

Through this series of special topics, With Red also hopes to present the true experience of "menstruation on the front line" for medical staff. Using real voices, we who are conducting the interview at the moment, and you who are reading in front of the screen, can discover the process, challenges, and difficulties of workers in different professions in dealing with menstruation on a daily basis.

In the future, be it in the medical field or daily life, when you find someone who is uncomfortable from menstrual cramps and needs a little relief, let us try to deal with it in a more empathetic, friendly manner together.

We are grateful to every medical staff member for their efforts. Their effort ensures normalcy and peace. I am also very grateful to the medical staff who were interviewed for sharing their menstrual experiences with us despite their busy schedules. From now on, let us be empathetic towards the very difficult and challenging daily lives that medical personnel face. We hope that more people will pay attention to the menstrual rights of medical personnel! We look forward to a day in the near future where everyone will no longer be hindered by menstruation.

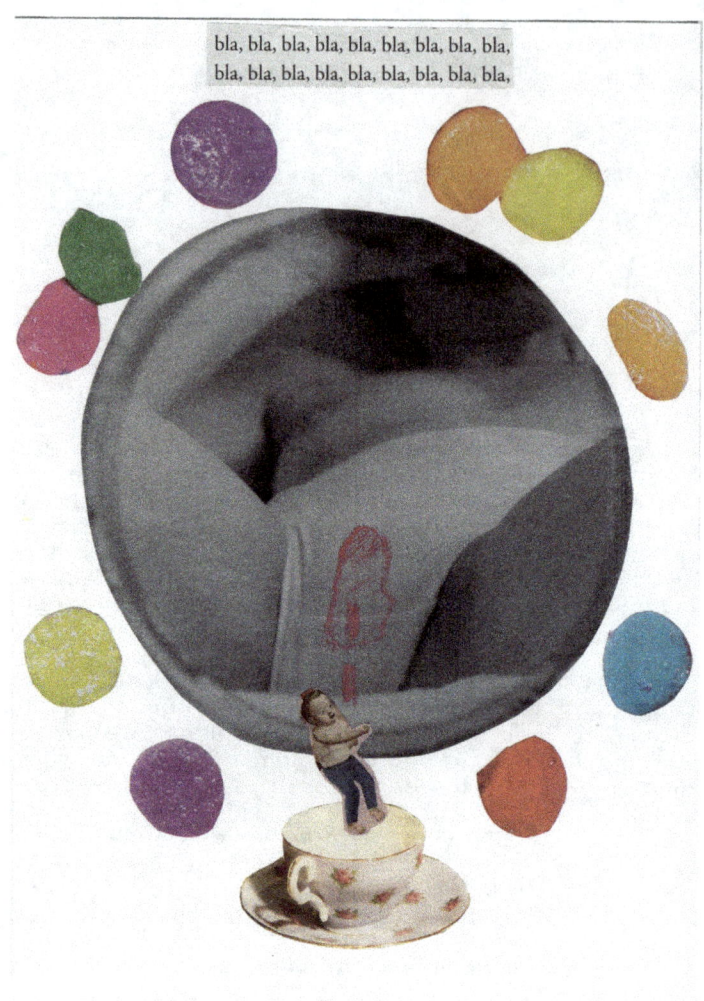

bla, bla, bla, bla, bla, bla, bla, bla, bla,
bla, bla, bla, bla, bla, bla, bla, bla, bla,

Isaienko, Yana (2022) - A "real" woman,
[collage]

Yana, a passionate artist from Lviv, Ukraine, began her artistic journey at age 11, initially exploring digital photography. At 14, she discovered analog photography, finding a profound connection with its unique charm. Since 2022, analog photography has been her primary mode of expression, enriched by her acting background which began at age 8. Yana's work often features self-portraits, blending theatrical experience with visual storytelling.

Driven by emotions surrounding the ongoing war in Ukraine, Yana expanded into collage art, creating poignant visual narratives. In 2022, she honed her skills through an online mentoring program with OdesaPhotoDays, developing the "Morning News" series under the guidance of Taras Buchko.

In 2023, Yana showcased her work at the Next Festival exhibition, hosted by Deutscher Jugend Fotopreis. As she continues to grow, she explores analog printing and seeks new collaborations, constantly evolving her artistic practice.

Menstrual equity is the ground we all need to stand on.

Jennifer Weiss-Wolf

visit the
exhibition

Explore more at:
starvingartist.cargo.site/blood-stains-
like-ink

ArtSteps: Blood Stains Like Ink

featured artists

Meg Wolensky | Philadelphia, PA, USA |
@aantics

Alexandra Low | San Jose, CA, USA |
@alexandrarlowauthor

F. Nadi | Leamington Spa, England

Yuying Huang| Shanghai, China | @yuyinghhhh

Isabella Covert | Savannah, GA, USA |
@isacov.art

Ally Zlatar | Glasgow, UK | @allyzlatar

Fred Fabre | Birmingham, UK | @nodaliter

Vasundhara Srinivas | New Delhi, India |
@vasundhara__srinivas

Yana Isaienko| Kyiv, Ukraine | @ysaienko

featured artists

Aubry Elizabeth | JBLM, WA, USA |
@aubryelizabeth.art

Kate Glass | Lincoln, NE, USA |
@kateglass.photography

Daisy-Drew Smith | Leicestershire, UK |
@daisydrew_art

Ye'ela Wilschanski| NYC, NY, USA | @ye.ela

Laetitia Heisler | Hamburg, Germany |
@laetitiaheisler

Madeleina Kay | Sheffield, UK |
@Madeleina_Kay

Izzy Sneed | The Colony, TX, USA | @izzysneed

Eszter Tunde Virok | Surakarta, Indonesia |
@misterjellyfish

Freya Fu | Los Angeles, USA | @freya_0413

concluding remarks

The pieces showcased in "blood stains like ink" remind us that the intersectional conversation around menstruation, bodily autonomy, and gender equality is far from over. The artworks featured in this collection not only depict the challenges and injustices faced by menstruators worldwide but also compel us to continue challenging the stigma surrounding periods and advocating for every person to experience menstruation with dignity and equality. As the conversation surrounding menstrual health, awareness and equality continues, we hope this publication spotlights some of the perspectives and opinions of menstruators and provides further insight into this pertinent issue.

contributors

The Starving Artist team would like to extend heartfelt thanks to our invaluable contributors, artists, and cover art artist **Kate Glass**. To our **artists**, your work transcends visuals or words; it is a profound reflection of lived experiences, unfiltered emotions, and a deep commitment to spark change. Through your art, you have helped us challenge stigma, foster understanding, and promote conversations that are crucial for menstrual equity and well-being worldwide.

In closing, for us it is not just about art; it is about empowerment, connection, and change. Together, we aim to encourage individuals to explore art as a systematic tool for highlighting the challenges of today in the hopes of creating a better tomorrow. We are truly united in our commitment to driving transformation within our society.

Thank you all!

Ally Zlatar and The Starving Artist Team

curator

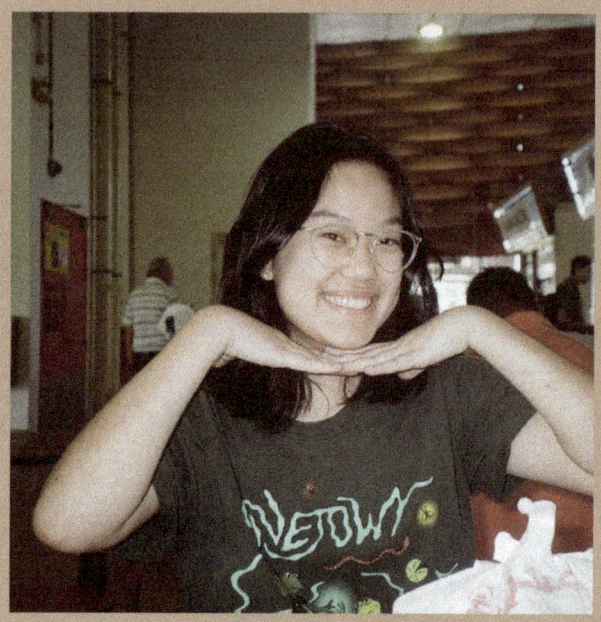

Gloria is a self-taught Singaporean artist who believes in the power of advocacy through artistic expression. Wielding a paintbrush and a catalogue of not-so-cryptic symbolism, she delights in the cathartic experience of art-making, with her work serving as authentic conversations on the never-ending search for purpose, her queer experience, and her mental health.

Now serving as a guest curator, she hopes to encourage viewers to empathize and resonate with the raw honesty radiating from each contributor's work and to interact with different facets of period equality and menstrual health.

Instagram: @gouachedaway

founder

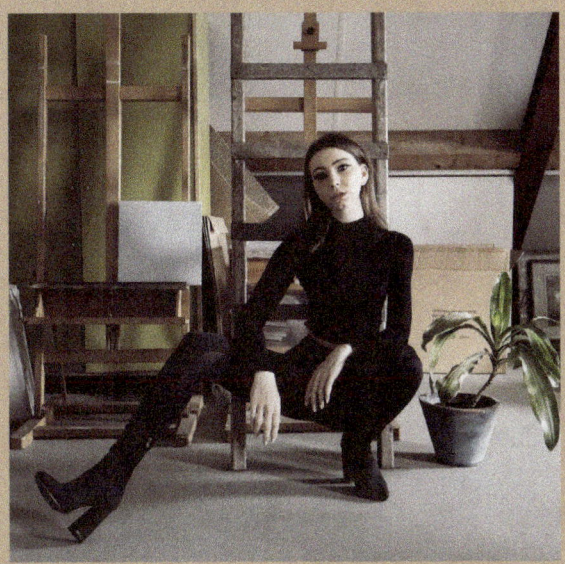

Ally Zlatar is an artist, scholar and activist. She is the founder of The Starving Artist; an artist initiative that utilizes creative voices as a way to create advocacy and systemic reform. She also founded The Starving Artist Scholarship Fund which helps people access inpatient mental health treatment. Her "This Body of Mine" campaign explores migrant experiences through creative voices and has helped support individuals and artists from refugee-seeking backgrounds globally.

Ally Zlatar has received numerous accolades for humanitarian work; such as the Commonwealth Innovation Awards (2023), UNWomen 30 for 2030 (2024), winner of The Princess Diana Legacy Award (2021). Her Doctorate in Creative Arts was completed at the University of Southern Queensland focusing on embodied experiences of mental illness in contemporary art.

Instagram: @allyzlatar

period partners

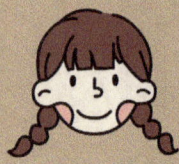 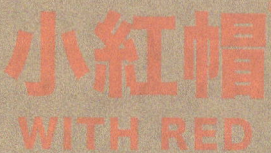 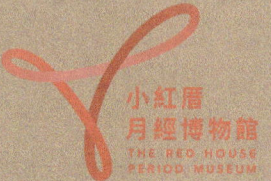

With Red & The Period Museum have impacted millions of lives globally since 2019. We are a highly recognized and influential Taiwanese NGO that advocates for period equity and addresses period poverty and stigma. In 2022, we established the world's only bricks-and-mortar Period Museum, The Red House, in Taipei, Taiwan.

At With Red The Period Musem, they believe that everyone shall rightfully own their true selves and have the right to live freely regardless of gender, identity, race or difference of any kind. We are committed to standing for diversity and inclusion and fighting for period equity and gender equality until those mentioned above become a reality for all.

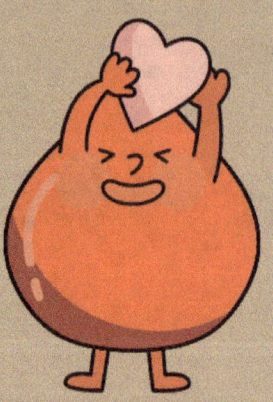

https://withred.org/

period partners

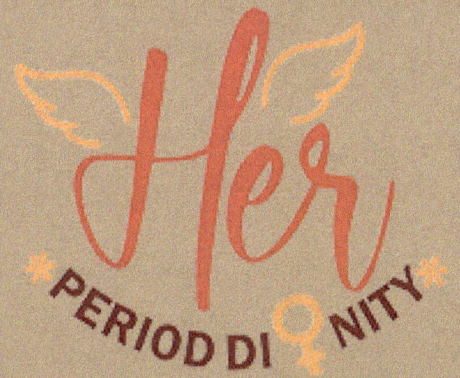

HER is committed to enhancing menstrual hygiene accessibility for women worldwide. Through fundraising, distribution, partnerships, and advocacy, they provide period products, hygiene education, healthcare, and sustainable employment.

They supply affordable and sustainable menstrual products, conduct gender-inclusive workshops to reduce period stigma, and offer free gynecological workshops to empower women with comprehensive health knowledge. Additionally, HER provides vocational training for former inmates to produce reusable pads, promoting sustainable income opportunities.

https://www.herperioddignity.co/

the starving artist

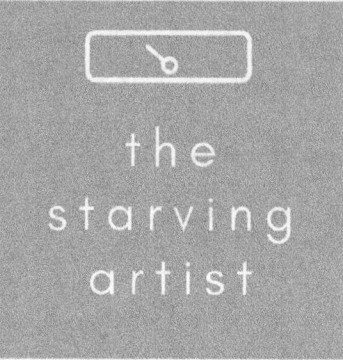

The Starving Artist is a platform that empowers individuals through the creative arts, emphasizing personal experiences. Our mission is to foster authentic and open conversations, aiming to drive change within existing systems. We particularly strive to support emerging voices in the creative arts, encouraging people to explore and express their experiences creatively. Our topics span various issues, including well-being, racial and gender rights, migrant experiences, and climate action. Through artistic expressions, exhibitions, publications, workshops, and collaborative efforts, we connect artists, individuals, and stakeholders to ignite systemic reform.

For more information visit:
https://starvingartist.cargo.site/

www.ingramcontent.com/pod-product-compliance
Lightning Source LLC
Chambersburg PA
CBHW071950210526
45479CB00003B/888